Autho

This book features 100 influential and inspiring quotes by Maya Angelou. Undoubtedly, this collection will give you a huge boost of inspiration and motivation.

1

"I've learned that people will forget what you said, people will forget what you did, but people will never forget how you made them feel."

2

"There is no greater agony than bearing an untold story inside you."

3

"What you're supposed to do when you don't like a thing is change it. If you can't change it, change the way you think about it. Don't complain."

4

"When someone shows you who they are believe them the first time."

5

"We delight in the beauty of the butterfly, but rarely admit the changes it has gone through to achieve that beauty."

6

"Courage is the most important of all the virtues because without courage, you can't practice any other virtue consistently."

7

"I can be changed by what happens to me. But I refuse to be reduced by it.

8

"I love to see a young girl go out and grab the world by the lapels. Life's a bitch. You've got to go out and kick ass."

9

"I don't trust people who don't love themselves and tell me, 'I love you.' ... There is an African saying which is: Be careful when a naked person offers you a shirt."

10

"I did then what I knew how to do. Now that I know better, I do better."

11

"Music was my refuge. I could crawl into the space between the notes and curl my back to loneliness."

12

"You may not control all the events that happen to you, but you can decide not to be reduced by them."

13

"Success is liking yourself, liking what you do, and liking how you do it."

14

"My mission in life is not merely to survive, but to thrive; and to do so with some passion, some compassion, some humor, and some style"

15

"Have enough courage to trust love one more time and always one more time."

16

"Never make someone a priority when all you are to them is an option."

17

"You may encounter many defeats, but you must not be defeated. In fact, it may be necessary to encounter the defeats, so you can know who you are, what you can rise from, how you can still come out of it."

18

"You can only become truly accomplished at something you love. Don't make money your goal. Instead pursue the things you love doing and then do them so well that people can't take their eyes off of you."

19

"A woman's heart should be so hidden in God that a man has to seek Him just to find her."

20

"Try to be a rainbow in
someone's cloud."

21

"You alone are enough. You have nothing to prove to anybody."

22

"The desire to reach for the stars is ambitious. The desire to reach hearts is wise."

23

"Ask for what you want and be prepared to get it!"

24

"If I am not good to myself, how can I expect anyone else to be good to me?"

25

"Stepping onto a brand-new path is difficult, but not more difficult than remaining in a situation, which is not nurturing to the whole woman."

26

"Everything in the universe has
a rhythm, everything dances. "

27

"No matter what happens, or how bad it seems today, life does go on, and it will be better tomorrow."

28

"Any book that helps a child to form a habit of reading, to make reading one of his deep and continuing needs, is good for him."

29

"You may shoot me with your words, you may cut me with your eyes, you may kill me with your hatefulness, but still, like air, I'll rise!"

30

"Bitterness is like cancer. It eats upon the host. But anger is like fire. It burns it all clean."

31

"Most people don't grow up. Most people age. They find parking spaces, honor their credit cards, get married, have children, and call that maturity. What that is, is aging."

32

"I don't trust anyone who doesn't laugh."

33

"My great hope is to laugh as much as I cry; to get my work done and try to love somebody and have the courage to accept the love in return."

34

"Hoping for the best, prepared for the worst, and unsurprised by anything in between."

35

"There's a world of difference between truth and facts. Facts can obscure truth."

36

"Love recognizes no barriers. It jumps hurdles, leaps fences, penetrates walls to arrive at its destination full of hope."

37

"Nothing can dim the light which shines from within."

38

"Let gratitude be the pillow upon which you kneel to say your nightly prayer. And let faith be the bridge you build to overcome evil and welcome good."

39

"Hate, it has caused a lot of problems in the world, but has not solved one yet."

40

"Life is pure adventure, and the sooner we realize that, the quicker we will be able to treat life as art."

41

"When you learn, teach, when you get, give."

42

"A friend may be waiting behind
a stranger's face."

43

"I've learned that even when I have pains, I don't have to be one."

"If you have only one smile in you, give it to the people you love. Don't be surly at home, then go out in the street and start grinning 'Good morning' at total strangers."

45

"I've learned that regardless of your relationship with your parents, you'll miss them when they're gone from your life."

46

"When I look back, I am so impressed again with the life-giving power of literature. If I were a young person today, trying to gain a sense of myself in the world, I would do that again by reading, just as I did when I was young."

47

"We need much less than we think we need."

48

"When we give cheerfully and accept gratefully, everyone is blessed."

49

"Surviving is important.
Thriving is elegant."

50

"Be present in all things and
thankful for all things."

51

"Without courage we cannot practice any other virtue with consistency. We can't be kind, true, merciful, generous, or honest."

52

"I sustain myself with the love of family."

53

"When we find someone who is brave, fun, intelligent, and loving, we have to thank the universe."

54

"First best is falling in love.
Second best is being in love.
Least best is falling out of love.
But any of it is better than
never having been in love."

55

"You can't use up creativity. The more you use, the more you have."

56

"Words mean more than what is set down on paper. It takes the human voice to infuse them with shades of deeper meaning."

57

"The problem I have with haters is that they see my glory, but they don't know my story..."

58

"The ship of my life may or may not be sailing on calm and amiable seas. The challenging days of my existence may or may not be bright and promising. Stormy or sunny days, glorious or lonely nights, I maintain an attitude of gratitude. If I insist on being pessimistic, there is always tomorrow. Today I am blessed."

59

"The ache for home lives in all of us. The safe place where we can go as we are and not be questioned."

60

"It is time for parents to teach young people early on that in diversity there is beauty and there is strength."

61

"I've learned that making a 'living' is not the same thing as 'making a life'."

62

"I am convinced that most people do not grow up... We marry and dare to have children and call that growing up. I think what we do is mostly grow old. We carry accumulation of years in our bodies, and on our faces, but generally our real selves, the children inside, are innocent and shy as magnolias."

63

"I believe that the most important single thing, beyond discipline and creativity is daring to dare."

64

"I've learned that whenever I decide something with an open heart, I usually make the right decision."

65

"All great achievements require time."

66

"Nothing will work unless you do."

67

"To those who have given up on love: I say, "Trust life a little bit."

68

"Each person deserves a day away in which no problems are confronted, no solutions searched for."

69

"In all the world, there is no heart for me like yours. In all the world, there is no love for you like mine."

70

"I've learned that you shouldn't go through life with a catcher's mitt on both hands; you need to be able to throw some things back."

71

"If you find it in your heart to care for somebody else, you will have succeeded."

72

"Anything that works against you can also work for you once you understand the Principle of Reverse."

73

"There is nothing so pitiful as a young cynic because he has gone from knowing nothing to believing nothing."

74

"Some people cannot see a good thing when it is right here, right now. Others can sense a good thing coming when it is days, months, or miles away."

75

"Instead, pursue the things you love doing, and then do them so well that people can't take their eyes off you."

76

"If you are always trying to be normal, you will never know how amazing you can be."

77

"Living well is an art that can be developed: a love of life and ability to take great pleasure from small offerings and assurance that the world owes you nothing and that every gift is exactly that, a gift. "

78

"If one is lucky, a solitary
fantasy can totally transform a
million realities."

79

"Success is loving life and daring to live it."

80

"Whining is not only graceless, but can be dangerous. It can alert a brute that a victim is in the neighborhood."

81

"We spend precious hours fearing the inevitable. It would be wise to use that time adoring our families, cherishing our friends and living our lives."

82

"My mother said I must always be intolerant of ignorance but understanding of illiteracy."

83

"You may not control all the events that happen to you, but you can decide not to be reduced by them. Try to be a rainbow in someone's cloud. Do not complain. Make every effort to change things you do not like. If you cannot make a change, change the way you have been thinking. You might find a new solution."

84

"I've learned that I still have a lot to learn."

85

"While I know myself as a creation of God, I am also obligated to realize and remember that everyone else and everything else are also God's creation."

86

"No one can take the place of a friend, no one."

87

"Life is going to give you just what you put in it. Put your whole heart in everything you do, and pray, then you can wait."

88

"When you wish someone joy, you wish them peace, love, prosperity, happiness... all the good things."

89

"Talent is like electricity. We don't understand electricity. We use it."

"To those who are given much,
much is expected."

91

"I believe that one can never leave home. I believe that one carries the shadows, the dreams, the fears and the dragons of home under one's skin, at the extreme corners of one's eyes and possibly in the gristle of the earlobe."

92

"Love life. Engage in it. Give it all you've got. Love it with a passion because life truly does give back, many times over, what you put into it."

93

"The sisters and brothers that you meet give you the materials which your character uses to build itself. It is said that some people are born great, others achieve it, some have it thrust upon them. In truth, the ways in which your character is built have to do with all three of those. Those around you, those you choose, and those who choose you."

"Love is like a virus. It can happen to anybody at any time."

95

"The human heart... tells us that we are more alike than we are unalike."

96

"Each time a woman stands up for herself, without knowing it possibly, without claiming it, she stands up for all women."

97

"While one may encounter many defeats, one must not be defeated."

98

"I believe most plain girls are virtuous because of the scarcity of opportunity to be otherwise."

99

"If you're for the right thing,
you do it without thinking."

100

"Live as though life was created
for you."

Made in the USA
Las Vegas, NV
26 March 2024

87627137R00057